u-Grand, Malume?

sizakele nkosi

Illustrations by Warren Jeremy Rourke

First published in 2023 by
Botsotso 59 Natal St, Bellevue East, 2198
botsotso@artslink.co.za
www.botsotso.org.za

ISBN: 978-1-990922-63-3

in the poems © Sizakele Nkosi
in the illustrations © Warren Jeremy Rourke

Acknowledgements:
Some of these poems in the same or similar versions have been published in New Coin, Tyhini and Years of Ash and Fire.

Layout and design: Advance Graphics

Cover: Advance Graphics using elements from "Poet's Sermon" and "Malume's Bones" by Warren Jeremy Rourke

Illustrations by Warren Jeremy Rourke:
    Malume's Bones A3. Watercolour – pg 6;
    Gog Sis Phakama A5. Watercolour and Fineliner – pg 14;
    Music Tour A5. Watercolour – pg 22;
    Poet's Sermon A5. Watercolour and Fineliner – pg 30;
    Meneputo Manunga A5. Watercolour – pg 38;
    u-Grand, Malume? A5. Watercolour – pg 53;
    Kasi Animals A5. Watercolour - pg 62

Illustration by Advance Graphics:
    Him – pg 46

for my uncle **Jabulani Maswanganye,** also known as
Jabu Mazibuko, who went into **exile** in 1977,
and disappeared without a **trace.**

CONTENTS

for my uncles (mandla and jabu) in exile	7
izint'eziphukile	10
translation of izinto'eziphukile: broken things	11
7 colors	12
consecration	13
gog'sis'phakama	15
full moon	16
sunlight	17
mama's story	18
pot plant	19
lord	20
ghosts	21
music tour	23
zwana mphefumulo	24
the music that keeps me up at might	25
to my BEE mzala	26
on the N17	27
the magic place	28
houses	29
poet's sermon	31
corner pritchard	32
naked	33
little girls' creed	34
woman in a red doek	36
here, roses must stand	37
meneputo manunga	39
gong-gong	40
translation of gong-gong:	42
six letters for 2016	44
responsory	45
him	47
first lesson	48
without wings	49
hawu baby	50
all kinds of joy	51
u-Grand, Malume?	52
june 16	55

i am my mother's daughter	56
behind closed curtains	57
kuhl'ukuthula – it's good to keep quiet!	58
things I don't like	59
rosary sessions	60
izilwane zasekasi	61
translation of izilwane zasekasi: kasi animals	63
today	65
glossary	66

for my uncles (Mandla and Jabu) in exile
after Ben J Langa – Staffrider, February 1980

malum' mandla, I found your children on facebook
nomagugu and themba
we talk now and then, share memories of you
pictures you carried when skipping the country
and the ones we took at your funeral

they were born in exile, still live far far from home
we will welcome them with a goat's bile one day
when history remembers unmarked graves

remember bra joe? i saw him at a funeral last week
he cried when he saw me, said i remind him of you guys
he said the last time he saw you, malum' jabu
your face was covered in blood, he thought you were dead

now let me update you with the news in dube.

sparks died drunk and broke
bra wandi runs a restaurant & bnb
other men are limping and stammering
loitering, raising grandchildren

i'm sure mdu last took a bath in 1982
when amabhunu hit his head with the back of an ak47
he walks around with pieces in plastic bags
doesn't have an ID   what can we do?

the moon remembers the day you left
when maponya sold the supermarket to shoprite
so many other spazas closed down and the pakistanis took over
it's still rough round dube hostel, they bomb atms, break into shops

makhedama is still there, still sells meat but also struggling
like the flower shop next to the butchery:
flowers shadowed by strands of hair
as litter grows from the ground

most neighbours have extended their houses
-3 backrooms and a garage
the apricot and peach trees are gone
all we have are broken streetlights and street humps

a lot of people you know have died
mlangeni passed on last year. they gave him a state funeral
the whole army was there
bra joe introduced me to some members
 "umshana ka jabu bob marley lo"
eyes running over me
they attended their drinks

can you believe tokyo married ingamla and left dube
I used to see his mother at fatima's
the time I attended mass every sunday

soweto can't afford electricity
people write their names down for food parcels
you loved this country so much that you left it
and what happened to the spear of the nation?
I wonder what was written in your letters –
a litany of dead or corrupt comrades?

all the letters you wrote from exile
how did you send them? because
we never received them

*

i can hear the fridge breathing and a soft soprano sound from outside
i hear mosquitos buzzing and a heavy silence from the walls

ama-apollo, moving cars and neighbours' windows
are disturbing the night's glow

the light on the ceiling burdens my eyes
i recall mom's memory of malum'jabu coming home

he used to leave a small bottle of umuthi outside the gate
so the police would only arrive after he had left

i go to the bathroom, lock myself in the mirror
pee and flush, go back to my bedroom
listen to running water fill up the bowl

i light my scented candle
think of all the ones i loved who died

i roll impepho into a stick
watch its smoke fill this old house

i fall on my knees and call my loved ones by their names
but ngiyangingiza when I want to speak to malum' jabu
what if he is dead? what if he is still alive?

Izint'eziphukile

ziyachichima izibaya ekhaya
ugog'uzethe zonke ngamagama

ngeliny'ilanga enye yezinkomazi
yaselwa ukubuyel' emzimkhulu
sayizwa impongoloza ngomlomo
mama! ayashis' amabele

ubisi lugcwele, ithole liyaf' indlala
ngicel'ungivulele salukazi
wavul'ugogo lathokoz'ithole
lathob'unina ngokulincela

salekelela nathi ngokulisenga
saluphuza lufudumele ubisi
hhayi ngoba ngiphuma phakathi'
kwezint' eziphukile

ngiphuma emanxiweni
emisamo edungwe yizivunguvungu
ezaleni - lapho abadala belinde khona
laph' abafazi beguqa ngamadol'aphukile

ngibazi kahle ubuhlungu
bokufelw' izint'ozikhonzile
ujeke lokufak' izimbali
izindaba zes'tofhu samalahle s'ka gogo

ngakhiwe ngomlotha
ngiphul'izinto yintukuthelo
hhayi ngoba ngiphuma
phakathi kwezint'eziphukile

Translation

broken things

kraals in my homestead
are overflowing:
grandmother has named them all

one day a heifer
was late to return to the great-house
we heard it bellowing:

mama! my teats are in heat

there is abundant milk
but the calf is emaciated

please let me in old-lady!

grandmother opened-up to the calf's happiness
it soothed its mother by suckling
we also helped by milking
drank while it was warm

no, i do not come out of broken things
i come from maternal quarters
ancestral altars dusted by whirlwinds
at the hearth –
the elders lie there waiting
while women kneel on battered knees

i know the sorrow of losing what i held dear
a vase in which flowers were kept
the coal-stove tales of grandmother

i am built of ashes
i break things
not because i come out
of broken things

7 colors

crystal white:
a well-made bed
a cup of rooibos
    mint leaves

passion black:
peanut butter & jam
teenage toddlers
    bodies and sweat

orange fire:
Matthew H
& the Gondwana Orchestra
    a tribute to Alice Coltrane

shades of blue:
Adelia's ex-voto poems
a man called X
the virgin mother and child
    the rivers of life

wine red:
lips
eye contact
heart
    olives and dark chocolate

mantis green:
God
grinds
    gold

magical yellow:
women of faith
Ludgardis and Christina
    night adder and a mole snake

consecration
to paballo

her breasts grow
her smell changes, shoulders shift
her face has woman spit on it
her lungs inhale more than they let out

she might not understand
why her lunchbox
has a foetus growing inside
with strawberries as a snack
or why inkomazi

is sometimes served as dinner

she begins to practice contrition
holy communion is her dream right now
this coming sunday she receives for the first time
sins   confession   absolution   penance

she prays:
let there be light on my tongue
may I find the perfect size for dancing shoes

she dances with eyes shut
arms stretched wide
the rhythm moving through her bones

she is a child of a thousand moons
hanging

gog' sis phakama

a gogo by the name of sis phakama
is the first to be called
when someone in our family dies
she understands death
washes those cold bodies
cries the most

gog' sis phakama was never married
spent many days imprisoned for shoplifting
one day, she wore inzila
as a disguise for her pickpocketing

diagnosed with hiv in her mid-forties
she got a dose of new life
at sixty-eight wears short leather skirts
manicured nails and organic weaves
enjoys six-inch stilettos

gog' sis phakama ends every family gathering
with a prayer
she prays for everyone one by one

on christmas last year
she prayed for mpumi my nephew
she asked the good lord to protect him
when he crosses koma road

inkulu baba somadla ikoma road, amen

full moon

your constant light flows
into unbalanced bodies
who search for God in theories

you stand close then high
confident the sun will rise
while I don't know who'll hold
my insecurities tonight
take all the hard pieces of my soul
make them soft again

I envy your completeness
you never take the shape of the stars
or mute your glow behind clouds

you are full in your moonness
while I beg sexiness from thick lips of men
and skin my happiness in desires
that like your's never outlast dawn

sunlight

i remember
the rusty blue kitchen cupboards
hanging on their hinges
the day my father left

it doesn't bother me much that
the president is on the news
promising houses, building ramps
for the disabled
and that people fight
for title deeds with witchcraft
-pain makes god-fearing people sin

we go through sundays babalazed
remember christ on good friday
singing for a moment

we offer ourselves up
because death scares us

we melt sunlight in a tin
for recycling purposes
wash our bodies with sunlight
mask our faces with sunlight

god shows up dressed in dirty flesh
distributing duplicate keys
to unlock heaven

mama's story

mama's husband died
in the arms of another woman
his body was found cold
on an eastern cape train-station
his liver had stopped working
mama arranged for his body
to be buried close to home

mama's sister dorah bled ceaselessly
in baragwanath hospital
her death was unfair to mama
it gave her six more children to raise

mama's brother mandla was assassinated
in washington dc
he was flown to south africa
in a beautiful american casket
buried in avalon cemetery
his grave has a black green
and gold tombstone

mama's mother died when i was six –
the apartheid police banged the door
so hard that her heart stopped

mama might have seen
her daughter mangi's soul leave her body
at the johannesburg gen
she was sitting in a wheelchair
smiling at mama
and then she closed her eyes

mama says if I wasn't around
she would have been dead by now

i am mama's beloved
her beloved daughter
beloved husband
beloved sister
beloved brother

pot plant

nothing ever grows in my home
except a small pot of coriander

barely surviving
on the kitchen windowsill
it spices the meat in the fridge

in my closet
i have pains neatly folded for morning

i mostly pick the ones that don't need ironing
so it's easier to be convinced
that i used to love you

lord

your Word oh Lord
has brought me shame

your wrath spreads across generations
with you, everything is wrong
even pleasure and passion

did the virgin truly want
to carry the child of man?
does the virgin have an opinion
on abortion or fantasize
about vibrating nipples
and milky breasts?

I am terrified oh Lord
your judgement and punishment
curse after curse after curse

I am terrified oh Lord of your love

ghosts

crawl in and out
of cracks across my bedroom walls
then roam inside my cunt

and every time I make love
they fiddle with my orgasm
fill the room with ex-lovers' rage

music tour

so where to?

dube station
via the main road
jozi fm on the left
-they play gospel and cheaters on thursdays
I bump into uncle ray next to the toilet
-they call the police station the toilet
he's from the gibson kente days
they used to gather at his home
not far from nkathuto primary
create plays and songs
now he exchanges lessons on g-scales
for a quart of black

hearty's fruit & veg is gone
-no one eats vegetables these days
behind it used to be bus terminals
hip hop was the heart of this place
mcs high on politics creating passionate verses
now it's a parking lot for sanele's tavern
my heart weeps

i pass the ashes of our theatre on machaba drive
stop by thebe lipere's jazz lounge
find khaya mahlangu jamming
with themba mokoena and some young bloods
they are serving butternut and spinach

so where to?

avalon cemetery
but i will not bother the dead
their bones are resting

as for their spirits,
those unquenchable spirits
still dance in the airwaves

zwana mphefumulo

1

mom and i enjoyed our tea
'zwana mphefumulo' between stories;

mduduzi ruined the song for all of us
God bless my mothers' sisters' eldest son
we die with laughter every time we get to 'mphefumulo'
he always goes off on some crazy key

'zwana mphefumulo' reminds us of our grandmother
i never got a chance to hear her sing it
but my mothers' soprano on those high notes
moves me

our neighbors joined in the music
ntate sechefu took us to the vatican
with falsettos and gregorian chants

we died with laughter

2

mom and i took a short drive to an open land
took a walk under the guidance of the sun
letting it set on our backs and eyes

i told mom about my vision
of a superwoman who smells like vanilla fields
we both paused and agreed at the same time:
Cleopatra

we found the perfect low hill
and spoke freely in unison
the open sky closed for a moment
then started to drizzle
we strolled back to the car
holding hands like lovers

the music that keeps me up at night

in the hours of dream

young voices dance
to the distant doef-doef
of senseless lyrics

drums chant ceaselessly
to izangoma who've woken
the drunken spirits of their fathers

at a night vigil,
the religious ones tap and clap
round a coffin in the bedroom

backroom tenants
discharge sexual screams
or are they violent ones?

my heart moves between keys
trying to find the right note

to start the day

to my BEE mzala

the humble four-roomed house
a toilet to the side of the yard
the one meal a day enjoyed on a plate of tears

hey, love
then time continued its ticking role
people grew into their predictable state
we started sleeping less
high on truths that kept rising
thanks to you, love
whose luck was never short of a miracle
loaves of rands stamped:
Black Economic Embezzlement

private school for the kids
house in a safe neighborhood
a car, a very plush and powerful car
the respect abo-uncle give you all the time
'coz now you give them hope for their next meal

you update your status
and thousands follow your check-ins to fancy bars
with men who are not on your son's birth certificate
also your daughter is experimenting with weed
sleeping on old men's chests
far away from the remedy she needs

i heard all of this at sparks' funeral
queuing for a seven-coloured lunch
on a random tuesday afternoon

hey, love
we are not sure how to greet you anymore

we are somewhere between chuckles and shame

on the N17

red and yellow plastic bag still in your hand
potatoes scattered across the road
a rainbow chicken tilted on its side
ready to boil with onions
but the freeway is for cars
where were you going?

soon there'll be phone calls looking for you
but now they'll have to identify your body:
arms akimbo, eyes staring into the bushes
body cold like the frozen pieces trapped in silver tinfoil
you bought for dinner
only to roast as hushed sunday lunch news

the magic place

in 1994
we used to put on our best dresses to go to the magic place
mine was sweet pink floral printed with lace layered underneath
lips were glossed up vaseline from a yellow jar
mine were shining from whatever i could find – fish-oil or glycerin
we used to walk with excited smiles to the magic place
find the magic man waiting with his box of tricks
we would be entertained, made into happy girls
having just seen a snake turn into a red rose
we'd clap our hands at the bird that lived in a box
and flew when called out by spells
we would save our amazement, store it in our hearts
use it when we really needed to dream

in 2012
i was sent to go call my dad from the magic place
i walked into a breath of drunken voices
staring at the father i couldn't recognize
i looked at the magic man
falling off his chair with a box of itakunyisa in his hand
the men gather here lately
to dull themselves with glasses of brandy
pain makes them look like boys who can't be sober
broken guitars playing redemption songs
to bring back their manhood
i walked out with boulders in my soul

houses

as a child
i used to notice peoples' kitchens -
if there were dishes in the sink
or izimfaduko eziclean

maseruto's house smelled of ice –
a mix of sugar and sixo
cabbage and amazimba from
the mini fruit & veg shop

ijaridi lakabo ntsumpa had tall grass
growing between ipaving
and there was always mud in that yard
from a burst pipe

what i remember about nonhlanhla's house
is that their gate was always locked
in later years, they installed a camera
and an intercom system

coming back home
mama and gogo's bedrooms
had two things in common:

ikhosomba – a thin corner between
the wall and wardrobe to stash
from umbrellas to blankets

and ilathi – a prayer table with the virgin mary
a candle, a flower;
a glow in the dark rosary

poet's sermon

dear faithfuls, snap your fingers –

a poet who lived in the time of eve
paints the garden of eden with images
every letter awakens the taste of apple water
music from solomon's song of songs

"sustain me with raisins,
refresh me with apples,
for i am sick with love"

the perfume of fresh flowers fragrant on the page
the poet touches souls with her lines
as the dear faithfuls remember to breathe

dear faithfuls, remember
                    to let your bodies breathe

corner pritchard

has a salon not much wider
than the backroom of a house
in mzimhlophe

a man selling imvunulo yesizulu
sits at the door
weaving coloured beads
into white tommy tekkies;
earrings, necklaces, belts, nezicholo
displayed on a small table

the guy who helped park my car
is shampooing another car
using water from a 750ml bottle
of sunlight dishwasher

the barber makes room
for a talkative drunken man
moves the damp towels
hairbrushes, blow-dryers
and combs from a chair
opposite the nail bar

i'm sitting on a crate
facing a mirror with a view
of people rushing, chatting
shopping, getting directions
smoking, busy on their phones

my hairdresser, his name is pat
pulls a needle from his pocket
sections my hair into little blocks
grabs one at a time
knits every strand
in-and-out, in-and-out
until it is dreadlocked

then he moves to the next block
    then the next

        then the next

naked

behind the opened curtains
my body in the window glowed
reflecting as does the moon

in the glass my curves
were a love story
composed by the sides of my womb

knees that kiss
do not always please each other
but they belong

on my heavy legs
below my dimpled thighs
there is a sharing of souls

paths on my belly
spread the pulse
to the rest of my organs

mountains guard my heart
soft rain gathers in my mouth
then storms out

love belongs in my heart
my body speaks the truth
i'm naked and flying

little girls' creed

1

the little girl from ghana has a big voice
she talks angrily when she speaks
she maintains good eye contact but never says much
since she moved to mzansi
her father has touched her body three times
the last time was really bad
her skin turned blue
now she wears the same blue dress to mass on sundays
watches her father pray at the foot of the cross
with ten votive candles shining on his face
she tries hard to remember the creed
goes to bed without food
but after a while she gives up on prayer, dreams of
making dresses when she grows up

2

there's a little girl in my english class
her father is in the sgb
everybody knows that he is unable to hold himself
he klapped a nun across the face once
now there is a rumour that
he is also free handed at home
his little daughter doesn't know where to look
every day she watches her father stand up
for communion during the weekday mass
she tries hard to remember the creed
-that god loves everybody
draws her mother's bruised body instead
at the back of her exercise book

3

another little girl came to school hallucinating
she thought death was following her
she found her mother drowning in the bath
the night after her father won the title match
against her mother's body
this little girl doesn't even try to learn the creed
she knows which number to call
when her father touches her mother's body
her creed is 911

woman in a red doek

the woman in a red doek gives me her back. her eyes staring at me
she is sitting on a bench. her arms stretching into fists

the woman in a red doek blurs out buildings with black windows
her eyes ignite flame in my eyes

the woman in a red doek is in the middle of the picture
the backdrop of the picture has a loud moving noise

the man in a black cap is cut off the frame
his body is absent, his lips half open

here, roses must stand

because the soil that buries
has also called me to plant
everything growing inside myself

if anyone should ask
where the lonely should rest
here, i will say

in case today becomes
a celebration of thorns
here, roses must stand

meneputo manunga

a !Xun san healer from angola
lived in plaatfontein
her home divided into three sections
a main sitting area and two bedrooms

bedroom 1 had an old DSAC branded curtain door
bedroom 2, a dirty-white cloth rolled and tied into a knot
all the windows were broken, walls painted in black smoke
floors felt thick and sticky with the residue of fire –
what can't be used to start a fire in this village?

meneputo manunga was one hundred and three years old
when paballo, nala and i met her
she told us about a little girl
who used to make dolls from mud

now this mud doll-maker couldn't bear children
her spirit guide told her to pour water into the soil
mix it till it smells like rain
shape it into a baby and place it in a green hut to dry

the next morning, she heard a little baby cry

Gong-Gong

Sivuke ngemvula today
ilanga beli-light-ile nje
sibong'ukugezwa ngamanzi
endleleni ebuy'eThongweni

bekunzim' ukushiya izingubo zam'ezishisayo shem
ngiphaphame lapho sesizoshay' i-roma khona
angazi nokwakwaz' ukuthi besibaleka siyaphi
mara besigijima – si-happy munt' wam'

saba semathandweni sina 17
sithand'ukufunda sonke
ngikuvakashela 'mang'buy'esontweni
ngigqoke i-uniform; ishirt eli-lime
green ne-skirt esi-navy
bengiyi-member yeFYC- Fatima Youth Choral
singcwab'abantu every saturday
ngikhenywa yiyoyonke into
ukufunana nama bare beige pantyhose
ukushelwa enye yasechoir-yeni abathi uStonto
ekhiph'umoya we-anyanisi nebhiya nge-baritone.
benginga-mind-i ukudoja imingcwabo
ngize kuwe malove-
bese ng'tshel'uMa ukuthi bekune-traffic emathuneni.
"if amathe nolimi was a person"
bengizifunela wena, mudemude wam' omnyama
sizifundelan' izinkondlo, sixoxe ngoSteve Biko
siblom' eRoots naseKhaya Lendaba kwaMkhulu Credo
lapho esafunda khona ukuphathana ngobuntu nangenhlonipho

Bengith'ufun'uk'shay'uvaye yazi
ngoba nawe mara X, bewungibiza ngoS'hlobo
uS'hlobo?
ngabona kungcono ngikhohlwe
into yothando kwasho ama2000s

"mjolo o tla go hurt-u"
Awuk'ufake u-m ku"ntwana" mawungibiza or
ungibize ngo "love" "mabhebheza" "motho waka"
ulibiza liphelele igama lam'
Awukaz' ungiqambel'amanga
Awukuz' ungishaye
Awukaz' ungi-rape-e
Awukaz' ungithuke
Awukaz'uyeke ukungifuna

and ngifun'ukuk'tshel'ukuthi
ngizwa ngathi kune *gong-gong* ngaphakathi kim'

ngafa ukumoyizela! ukukulangazelela!
mara umoya wam'ushay'umoya

Translation

Gong-Gong

I woke up with the rain today
the sun had just been switched on
I gave thanks for the washing of the body with water
on my way back from eThongweni

in my dream, I didn't want to leave my warm blankets
I woke up just before sishaya i-roma
I don't even know where we were running to
but we were running – besi-happy munt'wami

we first fell in love when we were 17
we loved studying together
I used to visit you on my way from church
-Jizas! my lime green shirt and navy skirt uniform
I was a member of the FYC: Fatima Youth Choral
we used to bury people every Saturday
I was bored by everything
the search for bare beige stockings
being shela'd/courted by uStonto from the choir
with onion and beer breathe coming out in baritone

I didn't mind to dodge the funerals
and come to you malove
then tell mom there was traffic at the cemetery
"if the saying, amathe nolimi was a person"
I just wanted you, my tall and dark love
to read poetry with you, talk about Steve Biko
hang at Roots and at mkhulu Credo's Khaya Lendaba
where we learnt to handle each other with ubuntu and respek

but at times I feared you wanted to do a hit & run on me
because you called me 'cousin', 'sister'
I thought it would be best to forget about love
as the ama2000 like to say, "mjolo o tla go hurt-u"
you never called me "ntwana" with an m
or "love", "mabhebeza", "motho waka"
you'd just say my name in full

yet you never lied to me
never hit me, never raped me
never cursed me
you never stopped looking for me
never stopped wanting me

so I want to say to you:
I feel a gong-gong inside my body
smiles are killing me
longing is killing me
though my spirit is calm

six letters for 2016

to my little brother:

you came into this world
when freedom was a breath away
we held you as fulfillment
of answered prayers
suddenly we were allowed to dream

to my big brother:

i know what to look up to
and brother
you're the reason
we climb forbidden trees

to my daughters:

i don't expect obedience
be nothing like me if you don't want to
but bring to life everything
that makes you skip like gazelles

to my husband:

i'm not willing
to die before my time
without laughter
or writing a beauty-filled poem

to my fourth graders:

your hearts are more open than mine
and i cannot spell correctly
all the words on your spelling list

to my body:

you've kept me away from my grave
revealed my being through your weakness
i've pushed you more than my soul can bear

responsory
          after adélia prado

st anthony
please find what i'm looking for
you who are tireless
there with God
enjoying eternal happiness
'coz me i am tired
not sure if what i need is laughter
or money or a feeling of peace
between my husband and i
silence comes from anguished memories
chaos explodes from our tongues

st anthony
you who have compassion for the suffering
i am haunted by an unbreakable vow
i have children to raise, needs to fill
i have stopped dreaming
i wonder about my life at night
and the sin i always confess

st anthony I promise
i will light a votive candle
pray the mystery of the rosary
i will chant your praises, lover of the cross
servant of the Lord
please find me sure feet

him

the night becomes the dawn of my loneliness
my temptation
              my thoughts of him
while my body entangles around yours

yes, tonight will find us holding hands
my body tangled around yours
         as we try and glimpse the future

but his heart is pumping blood in my heart
tonight
        and every night

first lesson

ready for my first day of school
new blue tunic with a gold collar
and a saint matthew's badge
on my left breast pocket
i had a red and white suitcase
with my lunch, pen, and paper
packed inside

at the door
men in blue uniform came to
bang things in the house
-sideboards, wardrobes, cupboards, chest of drawers
 "ons soek jabulani, waar is jabulani?"
they hauled out a black and white photo
of malume jabu who i'd never seen enough
to remember his face

umkhulu mhlongo, the school transport driver
didn't hoot for me when he saw police vans
he just left me to learn
my first lesson in history and afrikaans
inside our four-roomed house

my teachers, the police
and gogo gasping for air

without wings

a person can get drunk
from drowning in thought

being a mother is taking pictures
of moments that make you cry

we leave our children uncleansed
because of the moon

the moon doesn't show up
on heavy nights

our scares make us laugh
we break into pieces

our shadow follows us
like an answered prayer

we scorch like fire
angels flying with burnt wings

hawu baby

she locks herself in the bathroom
sits closer to the toilet paper -
drops of liquid cloud her eyes

messages: we're in this together
images: women dressed in their skins
phone rings and she picks up

"hello love," says the voice
"hawu baby, baby-daddy!"
her face drowns

⁕

now she's on her way to outdshoorn
driving between mountains
diving into blue possibilities

esperanza playing the bass in the background
her eyes take pictures of flat views while
breathing the open air

she sees love growing in the garden
under lemon trees and sky roofs
between rosemary and spinach leaves

all kinds of joy

like that dawn on the freeway
breathing each other's breaths
my soft skin all over your macho

i looked out the misty window
dark so the stars seemed close
and you flickered like my little heart
while the floor made crackling sounds:
chocolate, poetry pages, all kinds
of wrappings under our feet

we spoke in smiles and giggles
reclined all the way down
and looking up, hoped the sun
would be late
to leave us to make the heat
between our bodies
last

then linger

u-Grand, Malume?

to jabu mazibuko

1

i was nine months old
in prison with my mother
on the dawn of a march
so long ago it has ceased to matter

my mother's heart broke
inside my mouth that day
i was feeding on her right breast
from 5am until 8pm

we were in a small holding cell
at the protea police station
our crime a letter we never received

malume you had written from exile
though not one letter ever reached us
the telephone didn't ring with your voice
but the security police detained us anyway
demanding we account for a body
whose bones we still wait to bury

my nappy rash worsened

if only mama knew your grave number malume
or the house number of your current residence

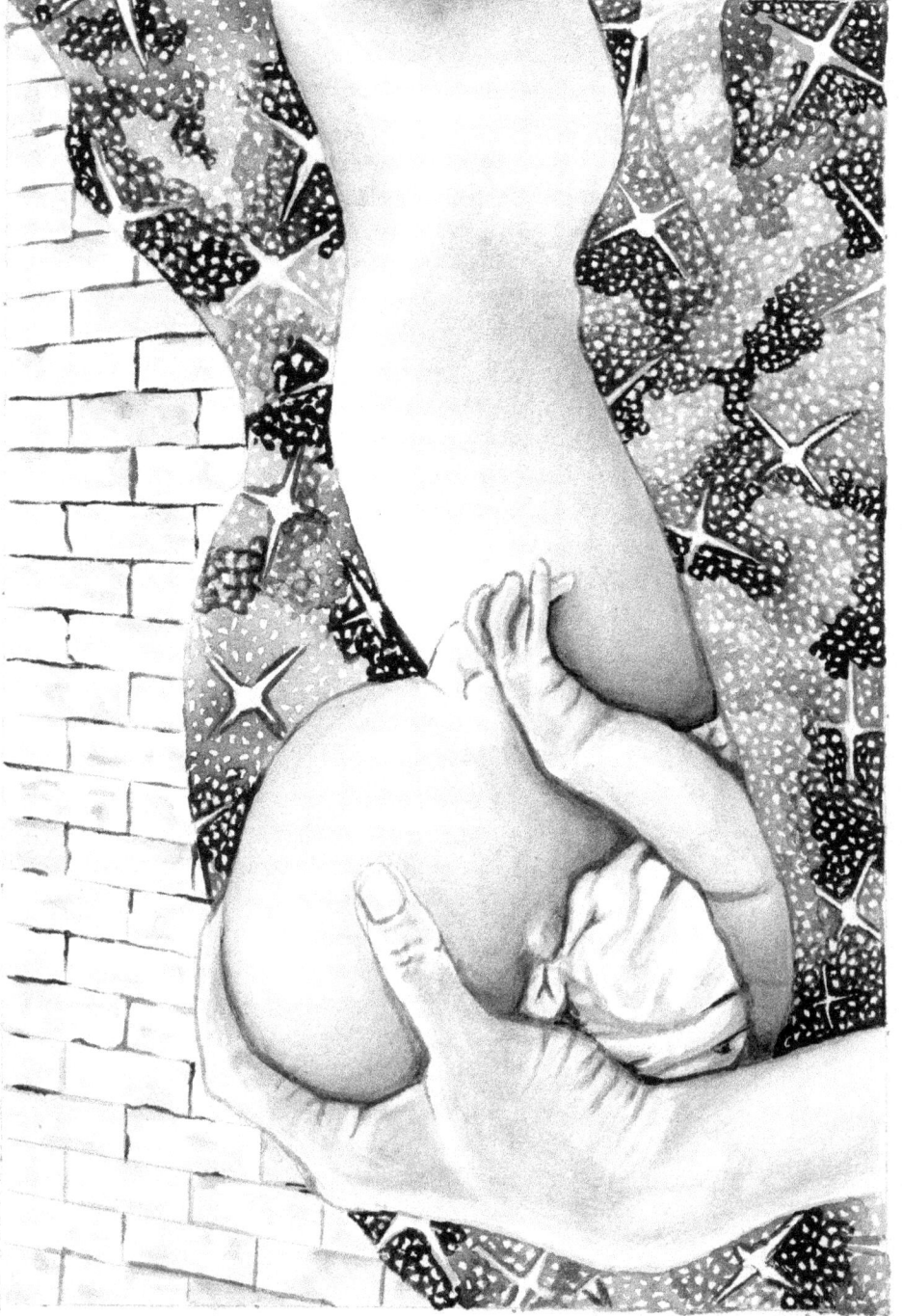

2

now i hear
you genuflect; kiss the bleeding feet of a white man,
you are drunk and guilty of his 'sins of the body' –
cunnilingus, masturbation, homosexuality . . .

you sit alone at a table, six bottles of corona on ice
staring at seriously sad-looking women dying of thirst
six sealed brutal fruits on a mountain of ice

you sleep-walk between taxi madness
smoke from chicken dust
lurch into the house of an angry wife

you drive around the whole night from one open spot to another
dance the piano drum line
until your sweat floods the floor

you lost your guns and boots
you lost your pen and children
on your way to freedom

june sixteen

the house i grew up in
hasn't changed that much
the kitchen is still the kitchen
only with running hot water now
the toilet still outside
in our backyard
the coal box still stands
packed full of magazines and pictures

after watering the garden
my siblings and i
fold the hosepipe inside
and cover the coal box
with a white cloth

when there's a family gathering
we sit round the coal box table
as if none of us has ever died

we welcome the departed from their graves
sing about their lives in songs
mama comes out from the main bedroom
june sixteen soaked in her eyes

mama tells us the story about mkhulu's funeral
that very same june sixteen of '76

mkhulu couldn't get to his grave that day
grandmother was alone with him in his coffin
while their three children were dodging bullets
holding fear in their clenched fists

we pray sorrowful mysteries
we beg the perpetual light to shine upon
the missing souls

the floors in our house have changed since
from carpets to ceramic tiles to wooden boards
polished reflecting flames of fire
like the youth of june sixteen

i am my mother's daughter

my father is a white ice-cream van
that he owns and plays jazz in
and drives away for weeks
rehearsing lines with his Kente friends
while I sit at the back seat
pushing back tears with my mouth
mama doesn't know that
udaddy dropped his pants
and left them on the bedroom floor
and ipenty lam' is on top of them
with blood stains

my father is the black suit
he wears and looks dashing in
the suit makes him look respectable
mama's heart hardens
and breaks and slits open her skin
that's how mama got that scar
on her face

my father is beautiful handwriting
he writes in cursive
crosses his dots t's and dots his i's
my father is a writer
he wrote all the letters we found
after umngcwabo wakhe
sifake amaroko a black
kungaphumi ngisho neliy'one
inyembezi

I wish I had a father
maybe I wouldn't have turned out
so hard and bitter
so fragile
and scared to raise my daughters

yes, it's too bad
I am just my mother's daughter

behind closed curtains

there is a room in our house
draped in red curtains

behind them is a box
covered in long silence

we never let the sun in

when night falls
we go inside the room
holding white candles
open the curtains for moonlight
hold the box very close to our hearts

and remember

kuhl' ukuthula – it's good to keep quiet!

izolo as'lalanga mina no-ma
we sang a duet of 'zwana mphefumulo'
decided to guide the prayer moment

both my brothers were out there
only God knows their phones were switched off
we calmed our spirits

mom showed me a new way
of kneading the scones dough
my first born managed the oven

we went out hunting for sharp knives
found an o-kappie,
sharpened it on the kitchen steps

my last born looked miserable
"mom, did you see there's a goat in the bathroom?"
"yes love, do you need to use the toilet?"

"no mama, it's just that the poor goat didn't make a mess
but you and gogo are busy sharpening your knives"
i chuckled and fetched a bowl to place the heart and liver

the men arrived after midnight
just as we got off our knees
hands red with animal blood

everyone ready after the wind allowed the fire to burn

things I don't like

1

The bloom of purple in kimberley
is cleo's vanilla scent
we met last night under the sun light
planting lavender seeds, singing
but izipoko zasekimberley uzizw'emoyeni –
malume's bones are buried inside my spirit
like cecil's inside his bronze-self on horseback –
there on some road island bordered by du toitspan

2

the sky in kimberley is pure
X calls me at 03.03
the moon is pink
white birds
draw a heart in the sky
three white birds
on each side of the moon

silence falls
I feel it in my womb
the night bird swallows the barking dog
the sun in my savannah is dry
a litre of water is R14.40

potholes
the big hole
there's no shortage of hell holes

rosary sessions

thursday rosary sessions
mama serves scones with butter, jam or cheese
her best tea-set, a white table charm
elegant yellow-gold designs
round the cups and saucers

>	she gave it to me as a wedding gift
>	I stopped using it, saved it from breaking.
>	my lover breaks glasses –
>	all my favorite wine glasses –
>	plates, mugs, my beautiful abusheni
>	he breaks them when washing dishes
>
>	mama's nicknames used to be pedantic
>	"sawubuna mntwana kaCondusive" OR
>	 "… have you spoken to *Palatable* about your piercings"
>	she cannot drink from plastic or glassware
>	chipped during dishwashing
>	thabo always rinses with too much force
>	bangs everything in the sink against the tap
>	so now the tap is leaking

hosting the statue of the virgin mother for a week
feels like carrying the crucifix and spring cleaning
the house before easter and christmas
the mystery of the rosary each day
the immaculate conception, the agony of Jesus in the garden
the holy assumption

>	i was taught to imitate the holy mother
>	so i did
>
>	the passion for christ
>	the sacred second sundays and the stockings drama
>	the blue and red sacred heart uniform
>	the membership fees and fundraisings
>	the sacred pilgrimages, the lent season
>	the color purple

Izilwane zasekasi

Ngizwe ubugudugudu ngabo 7 ek'seni
uPopi agijimisana nesilwane alandelwa uBoyzi
neskeem sakhe; babambe ama-pitbull ayi 8
uyabaz' abantu baseDube baneDrama kanjani
bebaqoqene ngamagroups; bagqoke ama-night dress
namagown -
wonk' umuntu usho eyakhe iversion yestory

uTutu ath' usibone kwasakuthanga lesilwane
sifana namagundwane aseAlex mara
sona sikhulu, cishe silingana nerabbit
besilokhu sijampa house to house -
from kaboMarushka. uDifa yena usibone la
egeyidini lakaboMajina
sadouble-up-a kwaZwane njengoba sesi la
kwaMlangeni.

Ubhut'Walter naye uth'usibonile isilwane
since sihlel'ebondweni ngabo 4 ek'seni
usibon' um'ebuya ezindaweni zakhe;
cishe esishisa nangamanz' abilayo

uRonnie ubusy ngapha ngeyakh'i-session
nabobaba bestradi bakhuluma ngezint'ezi-serious
"… singash'ukuthi siyi-symbol yobuthakathi lesilwane
Lesilwan' asinamsila… ende sifana nembiba
Sithunyelwe ngebulawo sizobulala lomphakathi
Imbiba phela yaswel'umsila ngokuthumezela"

Ngisalalele lapho sekukhulunya ngezimfene zaseZola
Usis'Khosi usiphethe ngengxoxo
Uthi izidididi zaseZola zi-hijack' itruck epheth'imfene zaseZoo
Somehow zaphum'imfene zabavoorvaya toe

ngakhumbula '92 kungcwatshw' ucomrade Mandla
kungcwela amasotsh'ashay'ingoma ukusuku bonke
bekuneGorilla edumile ekasi, ethand'ukuzula ebusuku
yatrapana neliny'isotsha etoilet ubusuku bonke – belidakiwe
ziningi isilwane ekasi angek'u-believ-e
ubuz'uSkhumba Hlophe
uzokutshela ngezikhova saseThembisa

Translation

kasi animals

I heard ubugudugudu round 7 in the morning
Poppy chasing an animal followed by Boyzi's
crew holding 8 pitbulls
you know the drama of the people of Dube!
gathered in groups, wearing night dresses and gowns
each telling their version

Tutu said she saw the animal day before yesterday
jumping house to house from Marushka's
it looked like the rats in Alex but bigger
almost the size of a rabbit

Difa saw it next to Majina's gate
it went through Zwane's pozzie
it's here now at Mlangeni's

bhut' Walter said he too saw the strange animal
sitting on the wall since round 4am
he saw it when he got back from his things
almost poured boiling water on it

Ronnie held a session with the men of the street
they talked about serious stuff
"… we can say that this animal is a symbol of witchcraft
it doesn't have a tail and it looks like imbila
it is sent with ibulawo to kill this community
phela imbila yaswela umsila ngokulayezela"

while listening to that I hear about the monkeys of Zola
sisKhosi says izidididi hijacked a truck from the zoo
somehow they escaped
now they are vuurvaaing them

I remembered '92, the burial of comrade Mandla
there were many soldiers, they sang the whole night
there used to be a famous gorilla
roaming round in the hood in the dark
got into a fistfight with one soldier in the toilet
the whole night he was drunk

there are a lot of animals ekasi
ask Skhumbuzo Hlophe
he'll tell you about the owls of Tembisa

today

my freedom still hangs on politics
of a country that has forgotten
that the dead speak

they let us out that night
but i'm still in prison malume

mama's breasts still bleed
i will feed on her left breast
until we can put flowers on your grave

GLOSSARY

Title   u-Grand, Malume? Are you okay uncle?

pg 7   bra — title given to a respectable man like "sir" or " prof"
amabhunu — zulu word for boers, also means anything that oppresses black people
spaza — a home-based or residential convenient store

pg 8   "umshana ka jabu bob marley lo" – "this is jabu, bob marley's niece/nephew"
Ingamla — white/privileged person
dube — location/kasi in Soweto
ama-apollo — high-rise streetlights

pg 9   impepho — helichrysum plant used to communicate with the ancestors, gods and god; burnt during rituals
ngiyangingiza — i stutter

pg 12   Matthew H & the Gondwana Orchestra – Matthew Halsall is an english jazz trumpeter, composer, producer and founder of an indie jazz label, Gondwana records. the gondwana orchestra is based in the UK, they play spiritual jazz and modern classics
Alice Coltrane — an american jazz pianist, organist, harpist, singer, composer, and wife of John Coltrane
Adelia — brazilian poet and writer
Ludgard — my grandmother's name
Christina — my mother's name

pg 15   gogo — grandmother
sis — short for sister
inkulu baba somadla ikoma road – koma road is huge Father, Great Father.

pg 17   babalazed — hungover

pg 18   avalon cemetery — one of the biggest cemeteries in soweto; many heroes of The Struggle are buried there

pg 23   jozi fm — a soweto community radio station

pg 24   zwana mphefumulo — a catholic hymn, 'behold my soul'

pg 25   izangama — a zulu word for spiritual diviners; derives from the word ingoma which means collective rhythm

pg 26	abo	uncles
	BEE	black economic empowerment
	Mzala	zulu word for cousin
pg 28	itakunyisa	tsonga word for " it will make you shit"; used to describe a very cheap drink
pg 29	izimfaduko	dish washing cloth
	amazimba	chips/crisps
	ijaridi lakabo	ntsumpa's yard
pg 32	imvunulo yesizulu	zulu regalia
	nezicholo	(zulu) hats; in older times, the word described a crown-shaped hairstyle indicating that a zulu woman was married
pg 34	mzansi	scamtho (a south african slang dialect incorporating many local languages) word for south africa
	sgb	school governing body
	klapped	smacked
pg 36	doek	turban/headcloth
pg 42	Gong-Gong	waterfalls in the northern cape, the only waterfall along the vaal river
	eThongweni	zulu word for resting place. derives from the word ubuthongo which means sleep that oscillates between dreams/visions and the realm of ancestors or collective wisdom of ancestors
	sishaya i-roma	scamtho expression for french kissing
	munt'wami	my love
	amathe nolimi	zulu) tongue and saliva; the idiom implies that people need each other, are inseparable, like the tongue and saliva
	mkhulu	grandfather
	credo's khaya lendaba – baba credo mutwa's village in Soweto	
	ubuntu	humanity; an African philosophy based on reciprocity and mutual respect
	ama2000	" the know-it-all generation" born in the 2000s
	mjolo o tla go hurt-u – dating will hurt you	
	mabhebeza	babes
	motho waka	Sotho word for my love

pg 50   hawu   an exclamation of surprise, astonishment

pg 57   Kente   Gibson Kente, father of popular Soweto theatre In the 1970's and 80's
         umngcwabo wakhe   (after) his funeral
         sifake amaroko a black – wearing black dresses
         kungaphumi ngisho neliy'one inyembezi – shedding not even a single tear

pg 59   izolo as'lalanga mina no-ma – mom and i didn't sleep last night

pg 60   izipoko zasekimberley uzizw'emoyeni – you can feel/hear Kimberley ghosts in the air

pg 61   abusheni   tsonga word for good day - a lifestyle brand by barman larry
         sawubuna mntwana kaConducive – greetings Conducive's child
         Conducive   name given to a mother who likes big english words

pg 64   imbila   rock hyrax
         ibulawo   bad spell
         phela imbila yaswela umsila ngokulayezela – a zulu proverb:
                                         the rock hyrax missed having a tail because of laziness
         izidididi   people who act foolishly
         vuurvaaing   causing havoc

Sizakele Nkosi is a poet and children story writer. Growing up in Soweto, she has been active as a facilitator of poetry and jazz sessions for many years through her platform, House of Siza. She currently works as a creative writing lecturer at Sol Plaatje University in Kimberley and is researching the life and work of Isabella Motadinyane, a founding member of the Botsotso Jesters. She is the co-host of the Art Lexcia Podcast and serves on the Culture Sector Committee for the SA National Commission for UNESCO.

www.ingramcontent.com/pod-product-compliance
Lightning Source LLC
Chambersburg PA
CBHW060839190426
43197CB00040B/2711